THE BEST TEACHINGS OF THE DALAI LAMA

Journey To A Happy, Fulfilling & Meaningful Life

J. Thomas

TABLE OF CONTENTS

INTRODUCTION

HAPPINESS IS ACHIEVABLE

Why is the Dalai Lama always smiling?

I'm sure I'm not the only one who's wondering. This is a man who has practically lost his country to another country. He is now living a frugal existence as the exiled leader of the Tibetans.

Why is this man smiling?

Anyone else would curl up in bed and refuse to leave. Others would sink into depression. There is no logical reason for him to maintain such as sunny deposition when everything he had has been snatched away from him. So why does he?

It's called happiness!

According to His Holiness the Fourteenth Dalai Lama, Tenzin Gyatso, when you're happy everything in life is bearable. It's not that he doesn't get sad, stressed or angry – but these are just passing emotions. When they occur he does not linger on them and instead replaces them with positive thoughts and happiness.

Happiness is not something that you feel when good things happen in your life. It is not something you feel when people say good things about you. It is not something you feel when you win an award. It is a state of living – present in grief or celebration, success or failure, stress or relaxation, suffering or pleasure.

It may look like a simple concept but a closer look at the thoughts beneath the glossy surface reveals some profound and real truths. For many of us – actually most of us - these truths are not that obvious. Rather than leave us floundering in the dark, the Dalai Lama has explored and expounded on the concept of happiness in many of his speeches and his talks.

This is not a course in Buddhism. In fact as you seek answers within this book you'll realize that Christian, Agnostic, Hindu, Muslim, Creationist, Pagan...this book applies to you, your faith and your life. This book is an exploration into the observations of a great man who has suffered just as we all do and gained insights from his experiences and life. He just happens to be a Buddhist

In his capacity as a leader, the Dalai Lama's mission is to guide people towards a peaceful and loving life, and to be the best they can be. His words provide timeless advice relevant to everyone; religious or atheist, Buddhist or non-Buddhist.

WHAT YOU'LL LEARN IN THIS BOOK

This book is stripped of all the complicated jargon and free of classic spiritualism. It unlocks the value in the Dalai Lama's words and interprets them in a way that the average man or woman living within a contemporary society can apply them into their daily life to achieve happiness, contentment and peace. This book will reveal:

- How suffering and happiness can coexist

- What true happiness really is and the difference between it and pleasure.

- Why loving-kindness and compassion are the entry points to happiness and how you can cultivate these concepts and apply them in your daily life

- How to ensure a better future for yourself with your way of living now

- Afflictive actions, speech and thoughts that may be causing you unhappiness and how you can wean yourself off these habits gradually for a happier you.

- What real wisdom is and how it affects your perception of your own suffering and other people and their actions.

- How to train your mind to reinterpret the things to happen to you in a positive way that will enhance your happiness

- Why you need to cultivate mindfulness and incorporate meditation practices into your daily life and how to do it so that you can increase your enjoyment of your life right now.

HOW TO USE THIS BOOK

Theories are good, but they're only worth something when they can be applied to your daily life. This book sets out Dalai Lama's teaching in clear actionable and achievable ways.

Within each chapter you'll find numerous tips about what to do in your daily life to apply the chapter. Nevertheless, I have also included some self-evaluation questions to help guide you on your journey to happiness. These questions will summarize the chapter as well as inspire you to act.

I advise that you read the whole book at least once just to get the general concepts within it then come back again this time with a journal where you can note down your reflections on the lessons you're learning as well as respond to the questions asked in the self-evaluation section. These questions are also excellent fodder for your analytical meditation sessions. They will serve as a good way to figure out your thoughts, emotions and deeds, as well as chart you future path.

This is a book for those who are genuinely seeking happiness. Hopefully by the end of it you'll have found numerous ways to encourage happiness, peace, calmness and positive emotions in your life.

Prepare to be happy!

CHAPTER 1:
SUFFERING & HAPPINESS INTERTWINED

Everyone wants to be happy. It is an immutable fact that we prove over and over right from the day of our birth when we cry because it's cold and we want to be warm. From then we spend every day of our lives looking for happiness and trying to avoid pain.

We go to school, work hard at achieving academic excellence and then do everything in our power to find a good job, not because it is simply a good thing to be a productive member of society, but because we want wealth. For the average person having our daily needs met is the equivalent of being happy while poverty translates to unhappiness.

We choose our life-partners based on whether they make us feel 'happy' and drop them if they don't. We exercise because we believe that good health and physical attractiveness will transform us into happy people while physical weakness will make us happy.

Seeking happiness is as much a part of being human as having a soul.

But what is this happiness we seek?

Is it being beautiful? Is it being healthy? Is it having a job that satisfies you both creatively and financially? Is it being able to put a roof over your head and food on your table? Is it having a partner who appreciates you for who you are and shows you that they do every day? Is it finally having children who are obedient, respectful and good citizens?

What if you have none of the above things, does that make you unhappy?

SUFFERING IS UNAVOIDABLE

If seeking happiness is an undeniable part of our DNA then suffering is the other side of the coin - some would say it's the ugly side. On the surface good health, beauty, career satisfaction, wealth, great family and social life etc all appear like the very definition of happiness. In truth everyone deserves a healthy body, a satisfying way to earn their living and a good support system. But the painful truth is that seldom do things work out so neatly.

Eventually all of us are going to experience grief, loss and sickness – if we're not already experiencing it. Why do you think there are so many self-help books? I bet if you walked to your local supermarket right now and to the book aisle you'll find a book for whatever is you dread ever happening to you.

Do you want your boss to never fire you? Here's a book for you. Need to lose those extra fifty pounds so that you don't keel over from a heart attack or have people sniffing at your as you walk by? Here's the perfect fat-blasting program for you. Want to make sure your ten-year old daughter doesn't get pregnant when they're just fifteen? Listen to this parenting guru. Do you want to guarantee that your partner will never look at another person? Here are quick tips.

But I bet you that if you go to copyright notice or the back page you'll notice a little disclaimer there stating that these tips may not work for everyone. Why? Because the creators of these books, speeches, articles, programs etc know that there is no fool-proof plan to avoid suffering. When it's your turn, it's your turn.

Don't be that person who is in denial. Some people in their quest for what they perceive to be happiness become extremely obsessed with perfectionism in every physical aspect of their life. They think that if they do everything right, that suffering won't occur. Unfortunately life comes with no guarantees and there are some types of suffering that not even shields laced with fire and poison can defend against. Eventually we all have to lose someone we love, spend time with people we dislike, not get something we want, lose something we value, get sick, age and die.

That's not to say that you shouldn't try to be the best you can be in all you do. My point is that you need to cut life some slack and realize that loss and failure is a part of it. Once you realize this then you can come up with strategies to deal positively with suffering when it occurs.

SUFFERING AS A SOURCE OF STRENGTH

When tragedy strikes, we react in different ways. Some of us fall into a depression whose length depends on the intensity of love for that person or object. Some of us turn to self-destructive habits as a means of masking our pain and finding some sort of relief from our pain. The best of us grieve over the loss but do not dwell on it. Instead we draw from our inner strength to help us move on from our pain.

But where does this inner strength come from?

Inner strength comes from previous suffering. It sounds like an incongruous statement but the reality is this; if you suffer now and survive it, it makes you better able to deal with suffering in the future.

Let me explain: I'm sure you know someone around you (or you are that person) whose earlier life was hard. Maybe they lost their parents when they were younger, they were born disabled, were poor. For some reason these are the people who are most likely to bounce back if something happens to them now. They seem like nothing can faze them.

Then take the example of a trust-fund baby who has been brought up with every privilege in life, never had any hardship or responsibility. When something happens to them or the things and people they love, their world crumbles. Put the 'sufferer' in the same situation and by tomorrow they'll have moved on from it or will be looking for quick resolutions to it.

The reason for this phenomenon is that suffering strengthens the human spirit with resilience. It is why parents are advised not to spoil their children but instead to give them chores, responsibility and curtail their access to leisure goods. This way you prepare them for those down-times in the future; time when things won't be so good.

It may be uncomfortable but some types of suffering, apart from increasing your resilience, also bear good fruits. Think of the pain a woman endures when she gives birth. The end result is a baby who is worth every contraction she suffered.

Consider work, which is a form of suffering since it requires that you exert and discomfiture yourself; we'd all rather be sitting at the beach watching the ocean. However suffering through early morning wake-ups gives you the pleasure of not just helping others with the work of your hands but also gaining your living.

SUFFERING DOES NOT MAKE YOU UNHAPPY

The good news is that happiness and suffering can coexist. According to the Dalai Lama it is not the situation that determines how happy or unhappy you are, but your attitude towards that situation. Your body can fail you but if your mind is right, it will not break you. Your family may disappoint you but if you have the right mindset you can still be happy.

The question then becomes; how do you even know that you are unhappy? These are the classic signs:

- You are withdrawn from people i.e. avoid them and even when with them set yourself apart instead of interacting

- Your thoughts are constantly on your problems, how dire they are and the things you do not have rather than on appreciating what you have.

- You brood to the point where you're constantly alone doing nothing but thinking over your problems and your productivity is very low. If you were to count what you did the whole day it wouldn't even fit on one hand.

- You are quick to anger. The smallest thing can set you off and you realize that people walk on egg-shells around you or avoid you.

You'll realize that nowhere there was did I say 'you have a problem' because we all do. We all suffer. How we decide to think of our suffering is what determines whether we are happy or not.

Happy people love to be around other people. They never seem to take anything too seriously and it is hard to draw them into an argument unless it is something they really care about – and even then they tend to argue it diplomatically rather than aggressively. Happy people take life's daily frustrations day by day and do not cling to others and their own past transgressions.

If you don't believe that suffering is not the cause of unhappiness then take a look at the people who survived the atrocities during the Holocaust. In most cases it wasn't the youngest or the most physically powerful who survived but rather those who purposed to survive. They decided that their situation would not break them. Even while their bodies suffered, their mind had already resolved to be strong. Happiness prepares you for the future and makes the journey through life bearable.

QUESTIONS TO THINK ABOUT

The worst experience I have ever had was when..... (fill in the blanks ex. Lost someone, something, got sick etc.)

- How did this experience hurt me?

- How did I deal with it?

- How did it change my attitude towards life?

- Did it change me for the better and how?

- Did it change me for the worse and how?

- Knowing what I know now, was this the healthy way to deal with my suffering?

- If the situation reoccurred today what would I change about my attitude and reaction towards it?

The greatest suffering I am experiencing in my life right now is...(Fill in the blank e.g. lost someone, something, lack of physical health etc)

- How has this suffering changed my physical environment?

- How has this suffering affected my attitude and feelings?

- How am I dealing with this suffering?

- Knowing what I know now, is the way I am dealing with this suffering healthy?

- What can I do to make my attitude towards my situation more positive?

CHAPTER 2:
THE TRUE MEANING OF HAPPINESS

What is happiness?

Before you can begin to seek happiness, you need to know what it is. For many people it is an amorphous concept marred by perceptions that have been built through time. Your parents tell you that happiness was having a good family and being able to provide for them. Your friends tell you happiness was having a beautiful partner and many friends. Your boss tells you that happiness is climbing the career ladder. Your image consultant tells you that looking good will make you feel good.

Are they all right? Are some of them right? Are none of them right?

The Dalai Lama has extensively talked on the topic of happiness and he emphasizes that none of the above perceptions of happiness are correct. Happiness is an attitude not an event. Let me explain:

HAPPINESS DEFINED

True happiness is not a product of the physical environment. It does not come from who the people around you are and what they do. It does not come from what you own. It does not come from the accolades you win or the events that happen around you. True happiness is innate and a creation of your mind. It is mental peace that can be achieved anytime, anywhere even when you do not have everything you want.

It does not matter whether sickness attacks your body. It doesn't matter whether your partner or children make choices that disappoint you. It doesn't matter whether you lose the ones you love, the job you love or other material gains. You can be happy despite all these events.

Think of the example of a rich man seated in his castle high up on the mountains and the monk begging for alms in the dirty streets below. It is completely possible, and regularly happens, for the monk to be much happier than that rich man. Why is it that some people quit high paying jobs to go into low-paying jobs or what others assume is menial labor? Because they are people who have discovered what brings them happiness and are willing to shed off the excesses of life to achieve it. Their choices may mean a different kind of suffering for instance a smaller house or less disposable incomes but the mental peace it brings far outweighs the physical suffering.

Many people focus on physical health and how to prevent or cure disease, assuming that having a strong body will somehow make them happier. While being physically healthy is a noble goal, happiness is not a factor of how healthy your body is. It is about how at peace your mind is and the resilience you have cultured in it. You can be happy even when your physical body is unwell but there is no possible way on earth that you can be happy if you are not mentally healthy. Furthermore while it is possible to prevent mental suffering, physical suffering is unavoidable – so why not focus on building your mental fortitude?

True happiness is unaffected by the external environment and the suffering that comes from it. It exists in you **in spite** of life's ups and downs - not because of them. It observes the nonsense that is happening outside of you then transcends and re-interprets them into more positive ways. True happiness is in the mind and finding it is all about transforming your intellect, emotions and attitudes. True happiness is mental peace.

HAPPINESS VS PLEASURE

Many people have the wrong perception of what mental peace actually is. Have you ever won something – a race, a trophy, a promotion? Do you feel that instant almost bursting out of your chest elation that had you smiling from ear to ear? For many this is the very definition of happiness – that momentary feeling that you are literally on top of the world. It is why you'll find people doing drugs, skydiving, drag racing or other actions that give them a rush and make them feel like they've conquered the world.

That's not happiness – that's pleasure.

Pleasure is an orchestrated moment of elation that is caused by what is happening around you; by the award given or the winning or the race or the birth of the baby. However when the cameras are gone and the trophy is just another bauble on your mantelpiece, the feeling is gone and you have to find new ways to reach that high again.

Happiness on the other hand is a state of being. You are happy washing the dishes, happy tending your garden, happy walking down the street and happy just sitting on the couch. Sometimes you may not even notice that you're happy because it is not an emotion that agitates the senses. Happiness thrives in normality. It is not something you deliberately set out to do. You can't say that 'at nine o'clock I'm going to be happy' and press a start or stop button. It is a constant and unending emotion.

Where happy people, though not abstaining from pleasurable moments ,will not make them the center of their lives, unhappy people will try to contrive as many pleasurable moments as they can in order to make up for the missing happiness in their normal life. The drunkard will keep drinking because the high makes his problems disappear temporarily. The gambler will keep throwing pennies down the machine because of that wonderful feeling they got last week when the bell rang for them. The debater will keep arguing because they love the feeling of winning.

We've already said that everyone is destined to suffer. However actively seeking pleasure tends to attract even more suffering then you're due. Drinking because you like the high will give you cirrhosis. Working too much for money or the promotion will lead to burn out and high blood pressure. Sexual immorality for the sake of fleeting pleasure will bring problems to your relationships as well as guilt. Pleasure may be fleeting but its consequences can follow you for much, much longer.

Now I don't know about you but I'm not looking for additional suffering. I'm happy enough with what I've got thank you. So how do you know whether what you are seeking is a pleasure that will bring you more suffering? By being conscious of what you are doing everyday and its effects on your long-term happiness. In later chapters we'll discuss how you can become mindful but basically every time you set out to do something you need to ask yourself:

Why am I doing this?

Will this harm my body, my mind or someone else right now?

Will this harm my body, my mind or someone else in the future?

These three questions will help you live a more conscious life and pave the way for true happiness. Apply these questions to everything you do – whether it is eating habits, chores, educational and career choices, family issues and you'll realize that decisions on what to do become much easier. You can focus on what you need rather than what you want; what will make you happy rather than what will give you pleasure.

ARE YOU A HAPPY PERSON?

A truly happy person accepts that suffering is unavoidable and inevitable but does not let it rule them or lie down and wait for it (thus unintentionally drawing even more suffering). Instead s/he has transformed their emotions and their attitudes towards this suffering and changed their way of living. The aim of these life-transformations is to ensure that they have peace of mind now, are prepared for their down periods when suffering will appear, and are able to bounce back from loss and sorrow quicker than the average person.

Where an unhappy person has let the things going on around them guide how they feel and how they behave to themselves and other people, a happy person has accepted that suffering is a natural part of life and has resolved not to let it define their behavior. Because they know that eventually they too will suffer traumatic events like loss of someone they love, loss of property and loss of physical health, they mentally prepare themselves to deal with these losses in a way that will allow them to get over the grieving process sooner and carry on with a happier life.

A truly happy person:

- May have problems but instead of brooding on how dire they are chooses to appreciate the gifts that they have and to focus on finding a solution rather than crying over the problem

- Does not make pleasurable moments the center of their existence. They may indulge in them but their objective in life is to make their daily life as happy as possible by transforming their thinking and developing the right mindset.

- Loves to interact with people with a spirit of sharing and giving. They are not afraid to show love and affection to others and seek ways to make other people's life better not hurt them.

- Is slow to anger but when they do look for productive ways to deal with the emotion instead of using words and actions to hurt the person who has caused it.

- Is not afraid to seek help from the people around them when their suffering overwhelms them.

In the next few chapters we will discuss the elements that enhance happiness or deter it but for now, I'd like you to consider whether you are truly happy. If you feel that you are now, do not despair. By the end of this book, you'll have found some strategies that can help you get onto the path of happiness.

QUESTIONS TO THINK ABOUT

I feel that the worst thing that could happen to me is......(fill in the blank ex. Losing someone, something, sickness etc)

- Why is this the worst thing?

- If it happened today what would I do?

- Knowing what I know now, would that be the healthy way to deal with it?

What is the difference between happiness and pleasure to me?

- Are there any pleasures that I have made at the center of my life to make up for the lack of happiness? (ex. gambling, sexual promiscuity, overworking, overeating, alcoholism, attacking others, etc)

- What have I gained from these pleasures?

- What have I lost from these pleasures?

- If I stopped seeking these pleasures would my life be better or worse?

- What will it take for me to stop indulging in this pleasure? (make a plan of attack)

CHAPTER 3:
LOVING-KINDNESS AS THE FOUNDATION

Regardless of social class, religion, political leanings, age, environment etc, everyone needs affection. Love is a fundamental human need. It's the reason why so many love songs are written and sang everyday and romance is the highest selling category of books. We are constantly seeking someone to show us love – sometimes in the right way and sometimes in the wrong way. Love is the foundation of happiness.

We've already said that everyone's primary desire is to be happy. Need for affection. Love and compassion are fundamental human needs. Why do you think there are so many love songs written and sang everyday – because we are constantly seeking someone to show us love and compassion. It is also the foundation for happiness.

This is why people who grow up in abusive or unhappy childhoods have trouble adjusting to relationships and sometimes end up closed off to others. They were denied their most fundamental desire and in turn do not know how to share it. A lack of love and affection leads to unhappiness. What most people do not realize is that to receive love and affection you must first show it to others.

Loving-kindness is the desire to bring other people happiness.

LOVING YOURSELF

Before you can show others loving-kindness, you should love yourself first. Some people see self-love as being a kind of selfishness. According to the Dalai Lama it isn't. You are just as human as the next person and therefore deserve love and affection from others and yourself. If you cannot show it the most important person in your life – you – how will be able to show it to others.

Self-love comes from first knowing yourself, your strengths and your weaknesses, then taking steps to remedying those things you feel you can change and accepting that which you cannot. Most people stumble when it comes to weaknesses because they obsess over the unchangeable especially physical flaws. The Dalai Lama advises that we think of our bodies as merely a vessel carrying the most important part of us, our soul.

Take an example of someone who is drinking milk. It doesn't matter if the cup is blue, white, slim, large, gilded in gold, glass – the milk will taste the same. However if you give him mud water, even a golden goblet will not make it taste like milk. Concentrate on filling your 'cup' with purity. The physical fades, changes, ages but the inside is constant.

That's not to say that caring for your body is vanity. On the contrary do what you can to enhance your physical health because your mind works best when you're healthy. However make sure that you have the right balance where your emotional and mental well-being is at the top of the list.

The weaknesses you should be focusing on are your personality weaknesses. Your reading this book is a first step towards that because it will challenge your concepts of good behavior towards yourself and other people. Learning about who you really are is an endless process but it starts by you being your own best-friend.

Treat and think of yourself as you would your best friend. If your best friend thought that they were not as good as that woman that just past by – what would you say to them? What are the characteristics that you would tell them made you want to be their best friend? Treat yourself with love.

The difference between self-love that brings happiness and self-love that brings suffering is if it causes others to suffer – then it is selfish. If your love for yourself comes at the price of other people then you can count it as happiness. For instance if you're seated at a table with five other people a cake to be between you; it is self-love to eat an equal share of the cake and selfish to take a larger share than everyone else. You are just as important and as unique as everyone else and deserve to be treated with respect.

Self-love extends beyond just thinking of yourself as worth affection, love and respect. It also includes self-forgiveness. Are there things you did in your past you still haven't forgiven yourself for? Maybe now is the time to explore them and forgive yourself. It is important to realize that you are only human. You are not perfect and you make mistakes – just like other people. When you acknowledge your own humanity and imperfection it is much easier to accept, forgive and love yourself and then in turn show that loving kindness to others.

If you've wronged someone else and haven't asked for forgiveness, it may be blocking your ability to forgive yourself because at the back of your mind, you're telling yourself you don't deserve it. Confess, apologize and make amends to those you have wronged. Do not try to excuse your behavior because that only makes it worse. Even for those who are unwilling to forgive your apology, just the act of accepting your faults and asking for forgiveness is purging.

Self-love does present an interesting conundrum. When you sacrifice yourself on behalf of others is this a form of self-hatred? According to the Dalai Lama it isn't. Self-love like happiness isn't about the physical environment, body or objects. It is about your inner life. You can sacrifice worldly wealth or undergo physical discomfort on behalf of others and still love yourself. The problem comes in when you sacrifice your peace of mind and happiness for the sake of others.

SHOWING GENUINE LOVE FOR OTHERS

While you cultivate your own self-love think of the people around you. They too deserve loving-kindness. Someone who has nurtured loving-kindness will be friendly and show a genuine and active interest in other people and their endeavors.

Take the example of the Dalai Lama who always has a smile for everyone be it the kings of the world or the beggars on the street seeking alms. He shows genuine interest in other people's opinions, struggles and their triumphs, praising them and encouraging them. When you have been in his presence you feel relaxed, happier and as if your self-worth has increased.

Loving-kindness is not only reserved for our friends and our families. You should strive to demonstrate it to everyone you meet, friend, stranger and foe alike. When you get on the bus or the train, do not ignore the person seated next to you. Even a polite hello and smile could make that person's day. Be caring of other people's well being and encourage friendship between you and other people.

BE NOT THE JUDGE

Love is the absence of judgment and it is tolerant. When you're a loving person, it does not matter whether someone is good or bad, poor or rich, old or young, blind or seeing, black or white, religious or irreligious...you understand that they are human too and deserve love and affection.

One of the greatest human deficiencies is perhaps our inability to accept each other as we are. We gravitate towards people who are like us and away from people who are not. We all have prejudices. When people are different from us in terms of how they think, dress, look, eat, worship, speak etc we find it harder to love them.

Understanding that at the core of it all we are all humans looking for happiness, love and affection will go a long way in helping you get rid of any prejudices you might have towards other people.

Disagreeing with someone's actions or beliefs does not make them less worth your loving-kindness. Everyone looks for their own road to happiness. Just because they're not following your path, it doesn't mean they're lost.

Someone loving will try to understand where other people are coming from with their opinions and actions even if they do not agree with them. You will see past the outward actions of the person and into the true motive of their actions which is the desire for happiness and for someone to understand them. Labels such as good or bad disappear and we start to see other people as human-beings with feelings, needs and desires and worthy of happiness.

SEEK INTIMACY

Everyone needs one special person who they can share their deepest feelings and fears with. This person may be a partners, friend, sibling or parent. Showing other people loving-kindness requires openness to and understanding of other people. But not everyone understands this and when you are undergoing your own suffering, they may not be able to reciprocate this loving-kindness.

You need someone who you can count on to give you this support during your own down times. You need someone who you always know will be there for you to provide you with the encouragement and affirmation you need during the time you are suffering and to celebrate with you when you triumph. Studies have shown that people who have intimate relationships are more likely to survive life-threatening illnesses like heart attacks and cancer and they are also more empathetic and compassionate to others.

The best confidants are those who support you but not condone you. A supporter will celebrate with you in victory and commiserate with you in failure. They will stand by you during your ups and downs. They are however unafraid to point out your mistakes and imperfections, and to correct you when you're out of line.

When you do find someone you feel supports you and you can confide in, they should see that they are one of the most important people to you and that you appreciate their presence in your life. If it means calling them more regularly just to check on them, telling them how you appreciate them, giving them gifts. Don't assume that they know how much you love and appreciate them, show it and say it.

In the same breath you should show them the kind of loving-kindness you would want them to show to you. As someone else's confidant you should:

- Support them in all their endeavors.

- Don't be afraid to tell them what you really think when they ask for advice

- Don't rub it in their face when you're right and they're wrong instead find a way to show that you support them despite their imperfections

- When they wrong you be quick to forgive

- Be verbal and actionable with your love and affection

When you show someone else loving-kindness, they instinctively mimic you. You will find that your relationships grow stronger. The more love you give, the more love you'll get.

QUESTIONS TO THINK ABOUT

Do I love myself?

- What character traits make me a good person

- What flaws do I need to correct myself

- Which have I worked harder to perfect? My body or my heart?

- Is this is the right balance?

- What am I going to do to create a better balance?

- If I were someone else would I be my best friend?

- Why would I be my best-friend?

- What is the worst thing I ever did?

- Have I forgiven myself for having done this act?

- The person I have really wronged is....

- Have I sought forgiveness for the way I hurt them

- Am I sacrificing my own inner peace in order to please others?

Do I show other people loving-kindness?

- Are people happier after they have been with me?

- Do I encourage friendship between myself and other people

- If I were in a crowded bus I would not want to sit near a.......(fill in a description)

- Why?

- Why should I sit next to this person anyway?

- What other prejudices and biases do I have against other people?

- Is there anything I can do to get rid of these biases?

- What can I do to show more loving-kindness to my family, friends, enemies and strangers and to encourage friendship?

Do I have a close and trusted confidant?

- Who is he or she?

- Why do I consider this person my confidant i.e. what about their behavior has made me feel like they support me?

- Am I reciprocating the same support to them?

- Are there ways I can be a better confidant to them?

CHAPTER 4:
COMPASSION AS THE CORNERSTONE

The difference between loving-kindness and compassion may be subtle but it is there. Where loving-kindness involves giving others happiness, compassion is more concerned with removing suffering.

Life is hard and many people are suffering sometimes by their own actions and sometimes because suffering is just part of the human condition. According to the Dalai Lama compassion and working to remove suffering from other people is a way of enhancing your own happiness.

EMPATHY AS THE GATEWAY TO COMPASSION

At the heart of compassion is the ability to put yourself in other people's shoes and tempering your reactions to them through empathy. If you do not understand what someone is going through it is hard to feel compassion for them. You do not want to be that person who is always telling others 'I wish you would just get over it already'.

Though suffering enhances your resilience, it might also increase your chances of dismissing other people's suffering because you have experienced worse and therefore do not see why this person is making such a big deal about 'nothing'. Then there's the kind of dismissiveness that is a product of never having experienced that kind of suffering and therefore you do not realize the extent of that person is suffering. Both are detrimental and you need to work hard to develop your empathy.

When people tell you their problems do not be dismissive of them and their feelings. Even if you think that this is something very minor, remember that to *that* person this is the worst thing that could possibly happen. Equate it to the worst kind of suffering you have experienced, draw from that pain so that you can empathize with this person. Listen to them, show them that you understand that they are suffering and are there for them.

Sometimes just this empathy is enough to alleviate someone else's suffering. When someone feels like there is someone who understands them it eases their own burden. Before you start giving solutions give understanding and empathy first.

SHOW ALTRUISM

In many cases, empathy is not enough. Compassion and altruism are inextricably intertwined, if you feel empathy for someone you will want to help them. True happiness comes from seeing that people around you are just as happy as you are. You become concerned with their well-being and want to remove their suffering according to your ability. Altruism is not grounded on pity. The person in need is not beneath you and thus deserving of your help. Rather your generosity is recognition that one day you too may need help but now that you don't it is your turn to help someone else.

It is also a way to release greed especially the possessive and jealous kind. When you are able to share those things that you consider precious to you, their hold over you diminishes. Unshackled by the love of possessions that have no meaning, you are free to search for a happiness based on love and compassion for other people rather than things. Interacting with those who are less well-off than you will also teach you to appreciate the little you have and not cast your eyes towards others' possessions. You should not give if you;

- Are being intimidated to give

- Are feeling ashamed of something you did and think that giving will somehow absolve you

- Expect that by giving you will get some kind of reward

- Want to feel good about yourself

Pure giving comes from a true desire to help others and not because you are expecting something in return. Make sure that your generosity is as private as possible, even hidden from the recipient if possible, because it then eliminates the expectation of a reward.

THE BOOMERANG EFFECT

The Dalai Lama says that compassionate actions are as much for that person and yourself as they are for the people around them. We are all inextricably intertwined and when your brother is suffering there is a boomerang effect to the people around them. When they are happy, the same is true.

Let's say for instance you know of an alcoholic in your neighborhood. You may think that that is their problem, but remember that they are not living in a vacuum and their actions are affecting others. His family may be suffering because he is unable to provide for them. Your own children may be watching him and glamorizing alcohol. The duties he performs at his work may be done shoddily and thus adversely affect his clients. If you help this alcoholic remove his suffering, you are helping other people too.

COMPASSION DESPITE BEING HURT

It is hard to be compassionate to people who have hurt you. According to the Dalai Lama, it is a necessary part of happiness. When you are truly compassionate, people's actions will not change the level of your compassion for them even when they disappoint you. Take the example of a married couple where one has wronged the other. If the wronged partner changes their attitude towards the wrong partner either by behaving angrily towards them then that isn't true compassion. When we genuinely care for someone, what they do does not matter.

That however does not mean that you become a doormat. You can still express your disappointment, just make sure that it is not in a way that is hurtful to them and that afterwards your behavior towards them does not change into either that of slander, anger or hatred. Obviously true compassion is not easy because we have been oriented towards personal gratification and acting out our hurt feeling. However, with continual practice you can develop true compassion.

QUESTIONS TO THINK ABOUT

Do I show other people empathy?

- When people speak to me of their problems how do I react to them?

- Do I listen to them and show understanding and commiseration?

- What can I do to improve how empathetic I am to other people?

How altruistic am I?

- When was the last time I gave to someone else outside my family?

- How did I help them?

- Why did I help them?

- Is this the right reason?

- How can I more altruistic – and in the right way?

How compassionate am I to those who have hurt me?

- Who has hurt me most recently?

- Have I been hurtful to them while expressing my disappointment in their actions?

- Is there any way I can show more compassion to them?

CHAPTER 5:
MORALITY, KARMA & THE FUTURE

Humans have been trying to define right and wrong since the beginning of time. Laws have been made, broken and changed all in the path to regulate human behavior. Here is a good example: Centuries ago killings in the name of religion were the norm and accepted. Slavery and racism was perfectly legal or 'right' and in fact laws had been to guide how it was done. Inequality between men and women was okay and inculcated in law.

Corporal punishment was the only way to deal with errant children. Homosexuals were at the bottom of the barrel. Sex was a taboo and assumed to be only for the married. The death penalty within the penal system was upheld. Come the twentieth century and things have changed drastically – whether for better or worse depends on who you're asking.

If we were able to time-travel to these times, you'd probably assume that people who perpetuated what we in modern times consider wrong were 'bad' people. But were they? The only people who can answer that are themselves. However, one thing remains true their behavior affected their happiness.

Morality and happiness are inextricably linked. Your perception of your own morality affects your self-love. When you feel you are in the wrong, it is hard to be happy because your conscience will keep pricking at you. Furthermore, your actions will also have consequences beyond the conscience prickling. According to the Dalai Lama, whatever you do will come back to you. Let's explore that:

WHO DETERMINES MORALITY?

Our society as a whole is fickle and our perceptions of right behavior change with the times and how we integrate with each other. However, change as there may be, our conscience will often tell us whether what we are right or wrong. If you always depend on laws of the majority to tell you what is wrong then you are risking your own happiness and morality.

According to the Dalai Lama, the conscience will always violently protest behaviors and attitudes that are not loving and compassionate. It does not matter what your religion, culture or background says. If the action you are doing violates your own or someone else's right to love and compassion then your conscience will protest it. These afflictive behaviors are:

- Afflictive actions i.e. killing, stealing, sexual misconduct, abusing intoxicants

- Afflictive speech i.e. lying, divisive speech, harsh speech

- Afflictive attitudes i.e. greed, anger, hatred

In further chapters we will discuss these afflictive behaviors. However, in general terms when we engage in these afflictive actions, our conscience is disturbed. But further than that we also risking our future happiness and drawing suffering towards ourselves. Which brings us to Karma!

THE LAW OF CAUSE & EFFECT

There are certain kinds of suffering we cannot avoid however by engaging in afflictive behavior we are encouraging more suffering than we are due in our lives. According to The Dalai Lama the things we say, do or think are inextricably linked to what happens to us in the future. This he calls karma.

Now you've probably heard about karma but I'll take a bit of time to explain exactly what it is and what it isn't. Karma isn't Fate. The two concepts are similar in that they are both concerned with what happens in the future. However where fate asserts that regardless of what we do, say or think, we all have a set path in life that we cannot change, karma articulates that our actions now determine our future and that is not set in stone.

Morality and our future path are intertwined. The natural law of cause and effect is that you do bad things and bad things happen to you in turn. Another difference is that karma is not fixed and unchangeable. It is fluid and changeable. The 'bad' choices in your past do not have to define your future. You are not fated to suffer unnecessary pain because of what you did. If you clean up your act, you can rewrite your future or change your karma. However if you continue doing what you're doing, inevitably you will reap the fruits if these bad seeds.

The problem with conscience is that if you continually ignore it, eventually it will keep quiet and. Karma on the other hand has no such qualms. It does not matter whether you regret doing what you have done or not.

In the next chapters we will be looking at each of these afflictive actions one by one and explaining how each correlates to your future. As you read you'll realize that by engaging in many actions, you are bringing harm to yourself even more than you are harming yourself. When your conscience pricks you, listen to it because it is saving you from unnecessary suffering.

Am I listening to my conscience?

- When was the last time I felt I had done something wrong?

- What did I do? Did I just ignore it or seek to make reparations to those I had wronged?

- If I didn't make up for it, what can I do now?

- In the future how will I make sure that this does not happen again?

- Looking at the laws in my country, which ones do I think are wrong, which ones do I think are right?

- Why do I feel this way? Is it because of personal prejudices or because I feel that they are not loving and compassionate to a group of people?

- Are there certain laws of morality I hold that are wrong and that I should be working to change?

CHAPTER 6:
OUR WORKS & KARMA

When we engage in afflictive actions such as killing, steal, sexual misconduct and abusing intoxicants we are drawing suffering into our lives. They affect our future and our relationships with the people around us. This is how:

KILLING

It's a pretty straight forward concept. If you snuff the life out of any sentient species whether it be through murder, abortion or suicide, your own life will be shortened whether it is through the sword/gun or by sickness. This rule applies even to those people who work with organizations whose products directly or indirectly cause death including drug and alcohol producers and the military.

It doesn't really matter what position you hold in these companies. Even the janitor at the bottom of the organizational chain is just as culpable as the head of the organization. For that reason it is important to scrutinize your job and who you work for to make sure that you are not unknowingly contributing towards death and thus sowing bad karma.

Most people forget that animals are also sentient species. We are not just custodians of ourselves but also of lower life forms including animals, birds and insects. The Dalai Lama advises that it is better to become a vegetarian or at least to reduce how much meat you eat to just the critical amount. He himself is an omnivore, but this is due to health concerns and as he says, he only eats meat when it is necessary which is every other day and in small quantities instead of everyday.

STEALING

If you take anything that is of value to someone else either without their consent or by deceiving them, then this theft will come back to you. Though it might seem like you have increased your own wealth, you are inviting scarcity into your life. Any projects you begin will eventually fail and eventually someone will swindle you too.

When we talk of stealing, it's not just snatching and grabbing a purse on the streets or holding people by gunpoint and ordering them to hand you their property. Many times stealing takes subtle forms. There are those people who take debts from other people or organizations like banks with promises of paying it back but never get to it. There are those people who encourage others to invest in their endeavors without giving their investors all the pertinent details that they know may deter investment.

There are those who do not pay all monies they owe the government including their taxes. There are those who will always find ways to avoid paying their bills be they telephone, electricity, water or other bills. Then there are those who believe that their employers have so much that taking something from the office without permission won't hurt them. It doesn't matter whether it is embezzlement, tax evasion or stealing printing papers, the result is the same. If you steal someone else's property, that property will not help you much and if anything it will affect your acquisition of your own property.

If you have been stealing in any way, your first action is to confess to what you have done to the people you have stolen from. Confession removes the burden of guilt that you have carried with you whether you know it or not. The next step is to return what has been stolen or make reparations for the damage you have caused. And finally – avoid any other incidences of stealing.

SEXUAL MISCONDUCT

According to the Dalai Lama all common sex acts that are between two consensual adults and do not cause harm to others are ethically acceptable. Though he does not believe in the concept of falling in love and soul-mates, he states that once you have chosen a life-partner, unfaithfulness, be it emotional or physical, will draw ill-fortune.

If you do not take care of your relationship, you will find yourself in competition with other men or women for your partner. The unfaithfulness you experience won't just be limited to your relationship. It will also extend to other areas of your life. You might find your business partners or other relations being undependable or disloyal to you. When they make a promise they will not keep it – just like you.

For unmarried people, the Dalai Lama encourages maintaining sexual purity until such a time as they find the partner they plan to spend their life with. His assertion is that sexual purity offers more personal freedom because indulgence in sexual pleasure usually breeds a bond that you may not be ready for now. If you want less problems with clinging partners until you're ready to settle down, then it is much better to abstain.

ABUSING INTOXICANTS

True happiness requires clarity of mind and equanimity. Intoxicants like alcohol and drugs blur our mind. When we are intoxicated our ability to interpret the things happening in our life and our situation is severely compromised because we cannot analyze them. They work on our physiology to lower our guard and thus ability to control our responses to the world around us. Take a look at anyone who is intoxicated; s/he is unable to control what they say or do to others making them less capable of showing love, kindness and compassion and more likely to hurt others.

Furthermore, intoxicants also ruin our physical health. The pleasure they provide is fleeting – most of the times less than a day – but they're effects last longer and cause even more suffering. Alcohol gives you a hangover, drugs cause withdrawal and those are just the short term effects. When used in the long-term, many intoxicant cause diseases to our organs and addiction.

The Dalai Lama does not indulge in the occasional 'glass'. His advice is to eschew it because you may be just one 'glass' away from all the detriments. It is never too late to stop. However, if you have developed an addiction and cannot quit your own, it is not shameful to seek help. There are many organizations and groups that can help you towards your path to clarity such as rehab centers. All you need to do is reach out for their help.

QUESTIONS TO THINK ABOUT

Have I killed in any way?

- Does the career I have directly or indirectly harm other sentient species?

- Do I sit back and watch while others are harmed without saying anything this making me an accomplice?

- If I have, how can I remedy the situation now and prevent myself from becoming any more complicit?

Have I stolen in any way?

- Have I stolen something from a friend, foe or the government?

- Have I manipulated someone into giving me something that I know they would not have given me if they knew the truth about what I really wanted to use it for or that I was not giving them the full value for it?

- Are there debts I have that I am not paying?

- How can I compensate those I have stolen from?

- How can I prevent myself from engaging in anymore thefts

If I am engaging in sexual intercourse, is my sexual conduct detrimental to me and my partner?

- Do I have my partner's full consent?

- Am I loyal to this partner?

- What can I do to be a better partner to them

Am I abusing intoxicants?

- What intoxicant am I abusing?

- How is this intoxicant hurting me?

- Why should I quit this intoxicant and are the reasons above enough?

- Why do I need this intoxicant despite the fact that it is hurting me?

- Is there a way to resolve the issues I have without taking this intoxicant?

- Will I need help to stop or can I do it on my own?

CHAPTER 7:
OUR SPEECH & KARMA

The tongue is one of the smallest organs in the body yet it can be one of the most lethal. A child will not remember the pain that came from a fall yesterday but they will carry the words their parents told them ten years ago and continue to mull over them and let them affect their lives.

Where not controlled, the tongue can ruin lives, relationships and friendships. Lying, divisive speech and afflictive speech not only harm those you turn your tongue against but also you yourself.

LYING

Do you lie about what job you do and what you earn? Do you lie about the state of your relationship? Do you lie about your real opinion about certain world issues just so that you can be politically correct? Do you lie about things you have seen, people you know or places you have been to just so that people can admire you? Lying is defined as the practice of giving others the incorrect perception of what we have done, what we have seen, what we believe or what we know.

This is perhaps one of the commonest non-virtuous actions that many of us commit. For some people lying has become such a usual part of their life that they do not even have to think about it before they do – the lies just flow out sometimes even when there is no need. Unfortunately, there is nothing that stays in the dark for long. Eventually people will catch on to your lies and the result is that no one will believe what you are saying even when you are being honest. To top on to that the people who are around you will also make a habit of lying to you.

According to the Dalai Lama there is only one good reason to lie. If it is going to save someone's life or prevent suffering. Many people interpret this to mean that if you know that the truth will hurt someone (even though they ask for it) we should lie to them. In such a case you need to consider the overall effect of your lie. In the long run will your lie cost their happiness or is it better to just tell them the truth now, hurt them now but let your truth help them in their future?

In many cases the truth is the best path, and where it isn't, silence is a better option. Let's say you are in a situation where you have been asked your opinion on a certain matter and you can see that the asker has already set in their minds what a 'good' opinion is and yours will only bring sharp disagreement. It is just better to say you prefer to keep your opinion to yourself. This way you are preserving the harmonious relationship between you and them.

DIVISIVE SPEECH

Where lying is saying something contrary to what you know and believe is true, divisive speech may be the truth or a lie but it is revealed in such a way that it will cause division between people. It may take on the form of backbiting, badmouthing or slander.

When you know that two people already have a discordant relationship there is no point carrying information between the two of them – telling them what the other said about them or the situation – because it will just stoke the bad blood between them. You are not showing love and compassion for either of them. Your role should be to broker peace between them not to widen the rift.

If you revel in others being in disharmonious relationships, your own relationships will become disharmonious. You will lose your own friends easily and will also become the subject of slander. Consider a situation where these two people or groups decide to mend their relationship, eventually your role in shuffling information between the two of them will be revealed and then you will become the enemy.

HARSH SPEECH

Lying and divisive speech often appear hand in hand with harsh speech. Harsh speech is where you deliberately use hurtful words to express your opinions. Harsh speech may take on the form of using a sarcastic tone with people. There are some people who just cannot reveal their opinions without implying that the person asking them is stupid for even asking the question. You may think that this kind of harsh speech is only limited to rebellious teens who when asked something answer in one word or roll their eyes as if the question is just ridiculous. It isn't. Everyone has done it at one time or another to someone we didn't want to speak to or had ill feelings towards.

Another form of harsh speech is when you deliberately pick on other people for their opinions, how they look or what they are doing. Have you found yourself making fun of someone's hairstyle or clothes or height or looks? You may think that you are just joking but the truth is that even though on the outside the person may smile, on the inside they have been pricked by your words and may harbor some resentment. You are not showing compassion.

Then there is swearing. Some people are already wondering what is wrong with swearing because in our society today it has become a common way of expression. Most people swear to express strong emotion while others swear to shock the people around them. The Dalai Lama teaches that strong emotions often lead to discordance and mar the clarity of your mind. Expressing it through angry words or violent actions only feeds it more and helps it grow. Furthermore to most people swearing is caustic to the ear and causes them to cringe because it is not a harmonious way of expressing yourself. Your aim should be to encourage peace and good feelings between you and the people around you.

The eventual effect of hurtful words is that the peaceful people around you will withdraw from you because you are seen as someone who is looking for a fight while those who are actually looking for a fight will be drawn towards you thus causing a lot of strife in your own life. If you think about what you're saying and watch your mouth, you'll find that your life will be more peaceful and happy.

QUESTIONS TO THINK ABOUT

What am I lying about in my daily life?

- When asked about my family situation, career, finances, background, opinion etc, do I lie?

- Why am I lying? Is it to prevent suffering of the asker or to because I feel that what I am is not good enough for them?

- What messages can I tell myself that will increase my self-esteem and reduce my need to falsify who I really am?

- Are there situations where I need to keep my silence rather than telling the truth?

- What kind of situations are these?

Have I engaged in divisive speech?

- When I realize that there is conflict between two people (or groups) that I am aware of, what do I do?

- Has what I have said hurt relationships between other people?

- What can I do in future to prevent myself from agitating the situation?

Do I engage in harsh speech?

- When I am stating my opinions are they said in a way that will build the listener or in a way that will irritate them?

- Do I make hurtful remarks about other people for how they look, speak, dress or think in the spirit of jest?

- Do I swear and why? Is it a shock tactic or just a normal way of life to me? Do I like the reaction that it inspires in other people or would I prefer to keep peace and harmony by modulating my speech?

- How will I control my speech so that it reflects love and compassion to the person who is listening to me?

CHAPTER 8:
OUR EMOTIONS & KARMA

Emotions are the hardest to deal with because more often than not, they are harder to control than overt action. You can keep yourself from hitting someone when you're angry but that does not mean that you are no longer angry. According to the Dalai Lama, even when not overtly expressed, emotions can be just as damaging to yourself and those around you. Seek to temper them or completely rid yourself of negative emotions.

GREED

A mother and a child walk into a toy store. The child spots a toy car and asks his mother if he can have it. She agrees and he rushes to get it but just as he is picking it off the shelf, he notices another car, this one bigger and shinier. He asks for that one instead. His mother after checking through her purse says that it's going to be a stretch but says okay. Elated the child walks with his mother to the payment counter. Just as his mother is paying for his new car, he notices another mother and child pair come over to the counter. The other child has an even bigger car that has rims his doesn't have and is driven by a remote controller. A fight erupts as both children start fighting over this bigger car.

We humans are like that child. We are never satisfied with what we have. Today we may think that as soon as we just get something we have set on our eyes on, we'll finally be satisfied. As soon as we get that thing we're elated – for about five minutes – then we start looking around for the next best thing. The problem with greed is that it is an emotion that is never satisfied. It thrives on the craving for more, more, more.

It can take on many forms. At its most basic it is the want for more even when you don't need it. You'll find someone with seven cars when they can only use one at any particular time, or a woman who has thousands of shoes some of which have never been worn or someone who will keep eating more food even when they are satisfied. You find yourself accumulating what you don't need to satisfy your hunger for more.

This kind of greed usually comes hand in hand with pride. Because you have so much you begin to feel that you are better than others and flaunt your possessions or qualities to everyone around you. If you're a good singer you expect to be the lead singer in every event. If you're clever you get into arguments with people just so that you can demonstrate how much you know. If you have a big house, you invite people over just so that they can see what a mansion you now have.

The problem with pride is that it inspires greed in others and desire for your possessions which can lead to the decrease in their own self-esteem, their withdrawal from you, their slandering you, or sometimes even their trying to acquire your possessions. If you find yourself talking about everything you have or showing off by being publicly generous instead of privately, then you have a problem with pride. To eliminate pride from your life, think of your shortcomings and all the things that you do not already know. By acknowledging that you are not the best at everything and won't be, you can deflate your ego.

The next level of greed is where you become clingy of your own possessions or personal qualities. You have a pair of shears, you neighbor asks you to lend it to him, you claim you're using them even though you're not. You refuse to invite people to your house because you are afraid they will eat your food. You know you can sing but refuse to sing at a friend's wedding because you feel they do not deserve your 'presence'. These are all forms of clinging greediness.

The final level of greed is the worst and most dangerous – when you discover that despite everything you have done, others still have more than you. They are wealthier, healthier, more intelligent, younger, more beautiful, more famous, more liked than you. Once you have cast your greed on others, it becomes unmanageable. At the very least your own self-esteem will plummet because you feel that they are worth more than you which can lead to depression or even cutting yourself off from these people if they are close to you. You may also develop jealousy and virulence towards them which you express by belittling them and/or their achievements through harsh speech, divisive speech or by lying. At the very worst you'll try to acquire what they have leading to stealing or sometimes even killing.

Greed is a very dangerous emotion that you should strive to eliminate in your life because the fact is that you will never have everything you want. When you are greedy, even those wonderful things you have in your life start to dim and not seem like much. Instead of obsessing on what you do not have and how to acquire more, focus on what you have and be thankful for it and on acquiring what you need rather than want.

Exposing yourself to situations that encourage comparisons breeds greed. If your friends are always talking about what they are going to next acquire or showing off what they have – it might be better for you to reduce contact with them until you have developed the ability to observe their possessions with equanimity or neutrality. Spend more time with those who have less than you. You will soon realize just how fortunate you are to have what you have and begin to appreciate it.

ANGER

Like greed, anger is one of the most damaging emotions. It is an uncontrolled energy that develops when you feel that others have wronged you. It eclipses your rationality to the point where you can end up saying or doing things that cause not just the person who has wronged you suffering but also increase your own suffering. According to the Dalai Lama there is no such thing as justifiable anger – anger is anger.

Consider a situation where someone close to you has provoked your anger. Your first instinct will be to say something scathing that hurts this person. A week later you discover that the person didn't deliberately set out to provoke you or wasn't even the one who did whatever angered you. Because you hurt the person, you now have to apologize. However even if they do accept this apology there may still be some remnants of the hurt you caused. Sometimes they may not even accept your apology. Because of your anger, you have caused unhappiness to both you and this person and damaged your relationship.

At that particular time when you begin to feel angry it may be hard to think clearly through the situation and realize that anger will not solve it. The Dalai Lama recommends that you remain silent until you are able to control the dangerous energy pulsing through you. Do not act or speak at that moment because your words and actions may lead to hurt. Concentrate on remaining calm. Withdrawing from the presence of that person may help but sometimes it is not possible. In that situation just remain still and silent. That immediate hot anger may take some time to abate but be patient. Your stillness may also give the person who has wronged you time to realize on their own that what they have done is wrong and apologize.

When you are finally able to think through the situation, start by admitting that you are angry. Don't pretend to yourself that just because you have not done or said anything, that the anger is gone. It is just cooler. By admitting its presence you are able to deal with it. Once you've admitted it, analyze its cause not from the eye of the person who has been hurt but like an objective judge. Anger is a self-defensive emotion so it can be hard to look at what has happened objectively. However once you realize that the person who wronged you has a background that has influenced their actions and deserves just as much love and compassion as you do and is probably also acting in self-defense it becomes much easier to look at their actions in a more compassionate way. Only love, compassion and understanding can neutralize anger.

When you are finally ready to talk to the person who wronged you, express your feelings in such a way that shows you are trying to recreate a harmonious relationship between the two of you, not hurt them. Instead of describing their mistake as something that defines them, express it as a hurtful action. For instance where someone has stolen from you, do not call them a thief instead explain that their stealing from you hurt you. They may then offer an apology and/or reparation, explain why they did what they did. You may even find that they felt like *you* wronged them and thus even require an apology from you. The result you're looking for in this conversation is forgiveness.

However if you feel that the conversation is once more leading towards division, step away from it and come back later. Sometimes it may not be possible to get an apology from that person but forgiving them is for your benefit as much as it is for their. When you carry unresolved anger, it transmutes into hatred - an equally dangerous emotion and potentially more destructive.

HATRED

Hatred is the point at which you begin to wish harm on other beings because of your ill-feelings towards them and revel in their suffering. It may be because that person has more than you in terms of possessions, physical attributes, talents or achievements and thus inspires jealousy from you. It may because you have been conditioned by your environment to think certain people are 'bad' be it because of their skin color, sexual orientation, past actions or physical features. It may because they have wronged you in the past and the situation between the two of you was not neutralized.

In some cases you may even think that you have a right to hate these people. You don't. Hatred is the direct opposite of love and compassion and has no place being called a good thing. It is everything love and compassion are not – it is not empathetic, kind, altruistic or tolerant and it leads to you losing love and compassion in your own life. People will not be interested in helping you just as you are not interested in showing compassion to the people you hate. It will not be easy for you to find love and people will not be tolerant of you either.

When your hatred comes from jealousy, spend time with those who are less fortunate than you so that you can realize just how much you already have. If your hatred comes from unresolved anger, seek ways to neutralize it including analyzing the cause of the anger and talking to the person who inspired it. If that is not possible then you need to talk to a professional or an intimate friend or relation who can help you let go of the past wrongs people have done to you.

If your anger comes from preconceived notions of who people are based on how they look or the choices they have made in their past, your best option is to spend time with these people and take the time to understand them. Let's say you have always believed that a certain group of people are cheats who will do anything to get your property. Deliberately cultivate a friendship with someone from that group of people. Soon you will begin to realize that this person is just like you with both virtues and faults and deserving of your love and compassion. The unfortunate part of this kind of hatred is that it is often fanned by stereotypes that are handed down generation from generation yet are rarely absolute. All you need to do is be around them and you'll realize it too.

QUESTIONS TO THINK ABOUT

Am I satisfied with what I have?

- Do I find myself constantly comparing myself to my friends and peers and think that I am better than them because of my wealth, relationship, talents, physical looks, academic achievement etc?

- Do I therefore flaunt my gifts and fake altruism so that they can see?

- How can I deal with this pride?

- Am I accumulating more wealth and objects than I need just to fit in with everyone else?

- Do I find myself constantly comparing myself to my friends and peers and think that they are better than me because of their wealth, relationship, talents, physical looks, academic achievement etc?

- Do I slander them because of this feeling of inadequacy?

- How can I deal with this jealousy?

- What do I have that I should be more thankful of?

- What do I really need in my life and how can I seek it instead of wealth?

How do I deal with anger?

- The last time I was angry it was because.....

- This angered me because...

- Was my anger justified? Why?

- How did I deal with this anger?

- Was it the right way

- How could I have dealt with it better?

- Am I easy to anger?

- Why?

- What can I do to reduce my irritability level?

- What will I do next time I become angry?

Am I afflicted by hatred?

- Who are my enemies?

- Why do I consider them my enemies?

- Knowing what I know now about love, compassion and afflictive emotions, is my hatred for them justified?

- Why isn't it justified?

What am I going to do to repair my relationship with this person or at least calm it?

CHAPTER 9:
WISDOM, EQUANIMITY & CLARITY OF MIND

If our state of mind is what determines if we are happy or not, then we should be taking every opportunity to develop, nurture and transform. Key to this transformation is the elimination of ignorance.

Ignorance may be defined as the act of holding wrong world views. When you perceive the world by eyes tainted by anger, hatred, greed and low self-esteem, you see yourself or others as less than human and begin to treat them as much. Ignorance inhibits your happiness because it eventually leads to the pursuit of pleasure or things we believe will assuage our feelings of hatred, anger and greed, as well as give us self-worth that we do not have.

The Dalai Lama classifies ignorance right at the same level with other non-virtuous actions such as killing, lying, stealing and hatred. He asserts that more often than not it is a lack of understanding of how the world and people are, that leads to the other non-virtuous actions. If you are wise, love and compassion come easily to you because you understand that people's actions towards you and others are influenced by their desire for happiness. If you are wise, you understand how karma and your morality are intertwined and will make an effort to keep from non-virtuous actions.

RECOGNIZE THE UNCHANGEABLES

To dispel ignorance recognize what you cannot change. The first step is towards that it to realize that **everyone desires happiness**. We may look for it in different ways sometimes destructive or not even know what it really is, but the heart of it is that everyone is just wants to be happy, to be loved and for someone to be compassionate towards them. When you understand this, dealing with people who've wronged you or have made wrong decisions in their life becomes much easier as your aim becomes to show them the love and compassion they are looking for rather than to condemn them.

We have already talked about realizing that **suffering is a fact of life** and something we cannot avoid, only reduce. Understanding that suffering is not just limited to you, will help you become more loving and compassionate to others as well as appreciate what little you have. Awareness the non-virtuous actions, speech and emotions that increase suffering, will help you achieve greater happiness as you find ways to avoid them.

According to the Dalai Lama, you need to also recognize that **nothing is permanent**. Today you might experience loss but tomorrow will be a day of gain. Today they may hate and censure you, tomorrow they will praise you. Life is a wheel that keeps turning sometimes driving you to the top and sometimes circling to the bottom. Suffering, like everything else, does not last forever. Change is as sure as death.

You also need to recognize that we are all **interdependent**. As sentient species we all depend on each other for survival. Just think of the circle of life. Soil breeds a plant, the plant is eaten by an animal, we eat the animal, we die and go back to the soil then the circle begins again. Even if individualism is so highly valued in the contemporary world, as humans we are incapable of surviving without cooperation and support for one another. I depend on you for love and compassion; you depend on me for love and compassion. If I destroy you, I am destroying myself and vice versus.

CULTIVATE EQUANIMITY

Understanding and acknowledging what is unchangeable completely transforms your perception of others, world events and what is happening to you. It allows you to see what is going on around you from an objective and neutral point of view. This unwavering neutrality is defined as equanimity.

When people wrong you, you realize that what they are doing is because they are seeking happiness but because they do not know what true happiness is, they end up seeking temporary pleasure or displaying non-virtuous emotions, actions or speech. You are then able to react in a just and compassionate way to their actions. When you endure personal hardship, it is much easier to survive and recover from it because you are prepared. When you have equanimity, you understand that sometimes it is necessary to endure pain to acquire happiness and thus do not avoid it.

Equanimity also connotes an evenness of your emotions. By this I mean that when you gain possessions or fame and are praised, you do not become overly elated because you know that eventually it will end. When you experience failure, loss and lack of recognition, you will not become overly depressed because you know that it cannot last forever. Eventually you will experience gain again. When you practice equanimity, your life is not ruled by the seeking of pleasures that give you possessions, fame or praise because they are not of true value to you. Instead your life is guided by the search for true happiness and the practice of love, compassion and wisdom. It is stability and stoicism in the face of fluctuations of your fortune.

Many people confuse equanimity for indifference or not caring about what happens. It is the exact opposite of that because equanimity is one of the highest forms of caring. Because you care so much about minimizing hurt to your fellow human beings, you always try to keep an even temper and not exploding in anger when dealing with others and make sure that all your actions and speech are geared towards helping them achieve happiness.

SCRUTINISE IDEAS

It seems counterproductive for the Dalai Lama to encourage skepticism after all most teachers consider their word as law and final but according to him his ideas are not written in stone. He does not encourage unquestioning and blind obedience to *any* rules because everyone has a background from which they are talking from and thus are influenced by it – including him. He says that you should scrutinize all teaching and ideas, test them against your own experiences and knowledge from other experts and see which ones apply to you and use them in your own life.

This skepticism should not only be applied to issues of morality and happiness but also to those that affect the world around us such as politics and governance, the environment, culture, education, health among other world concerns. We are all living in this world and therefore should be concerned with what is going on with it. Part of happiness is in remaining connected with it.

The Dalai Lama has on several occasions said that he is always open to dialogue about his own teachings. For instance on the issue of homosexuality, the he has expressed differing opinions several times on whether it is moral and immoral based on his talks with other people. Also, even though he advocates vegetarianism, he himself is not a vegetarian due to his health. To him, opinions are changeable and even teachings can transmute over time.

Like everything around us, our opinions on issues are changeable. Analytical meditation where you take some time out of the daily bustle of life to just think over these issues can help you determine your own perception of the teachings of the Dalai Lama and other experts. However, it is also important to discuss your ideas with people of differing opinions. The Dalai Lama, himself, has been involved in discussion on issues such as environmental conservation, communism and capitalism, education, the roles of men and woman. He never comes up with opinions without discussing it with more informed professionals.

When you put your own opinions to the test by interacting with people of differing views, you are able to measure their logic against yours and also make informed decisions about your values and the path of your life. Of course if you choose the wrong person to have discussions with – someone who is still influenced by the ego and wants to flaunt their knowledge rather than have a genuine exchange of ideas – the discussion may end up as an angry argument rather than a dialogue. So select someone who is of even temper like you for productive conversation.

QUESTIONS TO THINK ABOUT

Am I practicing equanimity?

- Do I get overjoyed when I gain wealth, fame or praise? Why?

- Why shouldn't I get overjoyed?

- What do other people say about my temper?

- What can I do to be more even tempered?

Do I scrutinize my ideas and perceptions?

- When people share knowledge with me (even those I admire) do I accept it as true or do I do I scrutinize it?

- What processes do I use in my bid to scrutinize new ideas I get?

- Do I maintain a close eye on the raging issues around me and have an opinion about them?

- What is my opinion on these issues? (Can be political, educational, legal, environmental issues its)

CHAPTER 10:
MINDFULNESS & MEDITATION FOR INNER PEACE

Inner peace is crucial for true happiness. In these days where being constantly busy is assumed to be the path towards success, it is increasingly hard for people to find inner peace and thus true happiness. Though it is hard to pull away from the rat race that is life, there are ways you can cultivate your inner peace; by being mindful and by meditating.

BRING MINDFULNESS TO YOUR DAILY LIFE

Lately the concept of mindfulness has become a buzzword. With so many people seemingly living individualistic lives that are on auto-pilot, the levels of dissatisfaction and stress have steadily increased over the years. By autopilot we mean that people hardly pay attention to what they are doing. Instead they think of what they did or what was done to them in the past, what they'll do in the future, and multitask to the point where the quality of their work suffers.

Mindfulness is about paying attention to what is going on around and inside you. When you are living a mindful life, you are thinking of what is going on now instead of what will happen in your future. For instance if you're walking on the beach, your thoughts are not on the troubles that you've left in the house. Instead all your thoughts are on the salty breeze flowing around you, the sound of the waves crashing on the beach, the feeling of the sand between your toes. You get to enjoy the moment despite everything that is going wrong in your life.

When you are talking to someone your head is in the conversation and that they are saying right then. You're not thinking of all the other things they've done in their past and letting these past actions color your perception of the conversation. When you're gardening, your thoughts are on the health of the flowers, the amount of water they need, which weeds need to be plucked and not on how you'll get to the office tomorrow morning and empty out all the cabinets.

Mindfulness reminds us of what is going on now. It is about focusing on the present, not the past or the future, and being aware of everything that is going on. Bring mindfulness to your eating habits, hobbies, work, mundane chores, physical sensations, relationships and you will begin to enjoy life now.

You will also be able to point out potential problems before they occur. Let's take the example of the two people on the beach. One is being mindful of their walk and noticing everything going on around her. The other is daydreaming and fretting about all the problems in her life. If something wrong would occur like someone with evil intent stalking them, who would be the first to notice? The same concept can be applied to a situation where you are in a conversation with someone else. By concentrating on what they are saying now instead of what they said last week, your reactions to will be more genuine, just and reasonable.

CULTIVATE THE MIND BY MEDITATING

Where mindfulness is concerned with how you live your daily life and paying attention to it, meditating is kind of a time out. You take time out of your day for personal contemplation. The Dalai Lama is an ardent enthusiast of mediating because it not only encourages mindfulness, but it also frees practitioners from mental obstructions and is the foundation for wisdom, equanimity and clarity of mind. By meditating we are able to consider the effects of our actions, emotions and speech and come up with effective ways to break free of destructive habits. We are able to contemplate the suffering we are undergoing and come up with healthy ways to deal with it.

There are two main types of meditation; focus of breath and analytical meditation. In **focus of breath** the person mediating concentrates on clearing the mind simply by listening to their breath. Thoughts may arise during this form of meditation, but they are observed then released. The point of this exercise is to quiet the mind and encourage you to become familiar with your body and mind.

This kind of meditation is especially important when you are experiencing negative emotion It allows you to calm down, concentrate on the physical rather than the emotional and let those difficult feelings go. However, even for those times when you feel stable, you should also practice it if only to train your mind on how to quiet itself.

It is not odd to notice pains and aches in your body that you've never noticed before. It shows that you have now become mindful to the state of your own body. The aches and pains may be a clue that there is something wrong with your physical health that you should take care of. Do not be alarmed if you get bored or fall asleep. The Dalai Lama has often said that sleep is the most perfect form of meditation since the mind is completely clear. The more you meditate, the more you'll acclimatize yourself to the silence and peace and avoid getting bored.

During **analytical meditation**, you are contemplating a particular situation, teaching or idea that you have experienced, heard or read about. Basically it is an internal dialogue with yourself where you go over this teaching or idea based on what you already know or have experienced and test its validity with the intention of either affirming it as true or rejecting it.

It is also during analytical meditation that you make resolutions about the changes you are going to make in your life to encourage happiness. Analytical meditation is best done after you have widely read on the teaching, thought or virtue espoused and also discussed it with someone whose opinion you trust and value. This way whatever you affirm or reject is based on knowledge rather than just opinion. When we meditate analytically we consolidate all we have experienced and learnt to achieve a deeper level of realization and wisdom.

In recent times, there has been increased interest in a **loving-kindness meditation**. If you read the section on loving-kindness then you know that it is the desire to bring other people happiness. Loving-kindness meditation is the practice of wishing others and yourself happiness, contentment and peace. In focus of breath you only clear your mind, in analytical mediation you contemplate ideas or events but in loving-kindness you focus on someone specific be it your friend, foe or just a stranger.

Knowing what you know about true happiness, visualize the person's face and wish them happiness. Loving kindness meditation may also include some chanting of all the things you wish for that person such as to receive loving kindness from other people, for his/her suffering to be more bearable, for other people to show this person more compassion etc.

Most people meditate in the lotus position. In full lotus, the person meditating will sit on the edge of a cushion with their back straight, place their left ankle on their right thigh and their right ankle on their left thigh. If you cannot do the full lotus, try the half lotus where you place your left ankle on your right thigh. Once in position, place your palms on your lap and keep your eyes closed.

If you're focusing on clearing your mind, concentrate on your breath. Notice how it goes in and out. Every time a thought crosses your mind try not to dwell on it and instead release and get back to focusing on your breath. Do this for as long as you have purposed to meditate.

If you're contemplating a particular teaching, begin by concentrating on your breathing then let the thoughts of the teaching fill your mind. Assume that you and your mind are separate entities and discuss and debate the thoughts you have on that teaching or issue. It doesn't have to be structured thoughts. You don't even have to come to a resolution within one meditation session. Just the process of thinking about it is beneficial and will help you come to a deeper realization. Back up your meditation sessions with periods of study during your normal day so that your mind is able to process and analyze the issue from a more knowledgeable point of view.

Make sure you've chosen a place and time when you are less likely to be interrupted. It should be the same place each day so that your psyche recognizes that it is meditation time each time you sit at that place. During the first few sessions, you might have a problem with staying still because we are not used to just stopping, so don't worry if you're fidgety. Instead start with little blocks of time. As the days go by increase your sitting time little by little until you reach your target amount of meditation time.

QUESTIONS TO THINK ABOUT

Am I mindful in my daily life?

- Do I focus too much on the past and the future at the price of my present?

- When I converse with people do I let their past actions color how I perceive their words?
- How can I live a more mindful life ?

Do I meditate?

- What time have I reserved in the course of my day for meditation?

- What kind of meditation do I prefer?

- How do I feel after a meditation session?

- What resolutions have I made at the end of my meditation session?

CONCLUSION:
START YOUR JOURNEY TO HAPPINESS
TODAY

I hope that this analysis of the Dalai Lama's teachings has helped you find the true path to happiness or at least given you a map towards it. True happiness is within your grasp. All you need to do is show true love and compassion to friend, stranger and foe alike by displaying loving-kindness, empathy, tolerance and generosity.

If you are already applying loving-kindness and compassion to your way of living, you'll find that it is easy to avoid afflictive actions, speech and thoughts. All it takes is for you to recognize that the person you are dealing with deserves love and compassion and to analyze whether what you are about to do will lead to their eventual happiness.

However, if you've realized that there are a lot of areas in your life that need tweaking then start with one afflictive action first. Let's say if you have some problems with hatred, gossip and stealing. Focus on only one – maybe stealing. Take some time out to fix this habit first even if it means seeking professional help. When you're comfortable that you have the habit under control, you can move on to the next habit and the next. Remember that karma is not an absolute and your past actions do not define your future unless you let them.

Cultivate wisdom, equanimity and clarity of mind by accepting and acknowledging the unchangeable facts of life, then applying them to your interpretation of the world and the people around you. Be mindful in your daily activities and meditate to encourage inner peace and also to achieve deeper realizations.

Finally, if you enjoyed this book, please take the time to share your thoughts and post a review on Amazon. We do our best to reach out to readers and provide the best value we can. Your positive review will help us achieve that. It'd be greatly appreciated!

But most of all – Be Happy!

Thank you and good luck!

A FINAL QUOTE

"We are visitors on this planet. We are here for one hundred years at the very most. During that period we must try to do something good, something useful, with our lives. if you contribute to other people's happiness, you will find the true meaning of life."

We wish you all the best in life !

Thank you and good luck !

Made in the USA
Lexington, KY
15 July 2015